THE CATHOLIC CHURCH HAS THE ANSWER

by

TAN

"Going therefore, teach ye all nations; baptizing them in the name of the Father, and of the Son, and of the Holy Ghost. Teaching them to observe all things whatsoever I have commanded you: and behold I am with you all days, even to the consummation of the world."
—Matthew 28:19-20

TAN BOOKS AND PUBLISHERS, INC.
Rockford, Illinois 61105

Nihil Obstat: Rev. Edmund J. Bradley
                 Censor Deputatus

Imprimatur: ✛ Timothy Manning
                 Auxiliary Bishop of Los Angeles
                 Vicar General
                 April 13, 1961

Originally published by the Loyola Book Co.,
Los Angeles, California.

TAN BOOKS AND PUBLISHERS, INC.
P.O. Box 424
Rockford, Illinois 61105

1986

THE
CATHOLIC CHURCH
HAS THE ANSWER

THE CATHOLIC CHURCH is the world's largest, and Christianity's oldest, religious body. Her 860 million members inhabit the width and breadth of the earth, comprising almost one-fifth of the total human population. She is far and away the most popular religious concept the world has ever known. Paradoxically, however, the Catholic Church is also the world's most controversial religious concept. Catholic belief is different, too different to be orthodox, say Protestants and Christian cultists. Catholic belief is too ethereal to be logical, and too strict to be enjoyable, say the humanists and agnostics. Hence to millions of people, Catholicism is not only a colossal success, it is also a colossal enigma. Of course, there has to be an explanation for these contradictory opinions—and there *is* an explanation: Protestants and others who have questions about Catholic belief too often make the mistake of going to the wrong place for the answers. Too often books written by religious incompetents are consulted. The result is incomplete and distorted information. With such information, one cannot help but see the Catholic faith as a colossal enigma.

1

The right place to go for information about Catholic belief—in fact the *only* place to go for complete and authoritative information—is the Catholic Church herself. As any detective will tell you, no investigation is quite so complete as an on-the-spot investigation. Hence, dear reader, if you are a Protestant, an unaffiliated Christian, or an agnostic, who wants to know the truth about Catholic belief, take this friendly advice: Seek out a Catholic priest and put your questions to him. You will find him a very understanding and obliging person. Or read this little booklet. This booklet was written by a Catholic who knows the questions you are likely to ask, as well as the answers, because once he, too, was outside of the Catholic Church, looking in. The questions in this booklet are basically the same ones he put to a Catholic priest, and the answers are basically the same ones given him by that priest. Read this booklet; then forget all the fiction you have heard about the Catholic Church, for you will have the gospel truth.

Why do Catholics believe that the universe and all life in it was created by, and is governed by, an all-powerful Spirit Being called God? What actual proof is there of God's existence and omnipotence?

Catholics believe that the universe is the creation, and the exclusive dominion, of an infinitely powerful Spirit Being, called God, because the evidence which points to that conclusion is so overwhelming that there is no room left for even the slightest vestige of doubt. First, there is the evidence of logic. Through the process of simple mathematical-type reasoning, man inevitably comes face to face with certain indisputable principles: Everything has a cause; nothing can bring itself into existence. Obviously there is a long chain of causes in the universe, but ultimately there must be a *first* cause, an uncaused cause. This uncaused cause we call "God." (The theory of evolution, even if it could be proved, would not explain the origin of anything; evolution simply deals with what may have happened *after* matter came into existence.) Further, 1) personal creation (man) presupposes a superior Personal Creator, 2) universal order presupposes a Universal Orderer, 3) cosmic energy presupposes a Cosmic Energizer, 4) natural law presupposes a Universal Law Maker. Basic principles of reason such as these explain why so many of the world's leading scientists are firm believers in God.

Then, there is the evidence of divine revelation—on countless occasions God has revealed Himself by voice, vision and apparition (by means which are receptive to the human senses), and demonstrated His Omnipotence by stupendous, obviously supernatural miracles. Many of

3

these revelations are a matter of authenticated historical record. The Scriptures, for example, are full of such accounts; and in modern times the world has been witness to such Heaven-sent miracles as those at Fatima, Lourdes, and St. Anne de Beaupré in Quebec, Canada, where the cured have left a forest of crutches in testimony. (The Lourdes Medical Bureau is open for examination by any doctor.) In addition, there is the liquefaction of the blood of St. Januarius which still takes place in Naples each year on September 19, his feastday; the incorruption of the bodies of many Catholic saints (such as St. Bernadette, who died in 1879); and the miraculous Eucharistic Host of Lanciano, Italy, which has been scientifically proven to be human flesh and human blood, type AB—to mention only a few of the miracles still on-going in the 20th century, which point to the existence of a God.

And lastly there is the evidence of human intuition. Psychologists have long known that every human being—the atheist included—intuitively seeks God's help in times of great calamity, and instinctively pleads for God's mercy when death is imminent. Hence the renowned Voltaire, who was so eloquent in his denial of God while he enjoyed health, fame and fortune, repudiated all of his atheistic writings on his deathbed and frantically sought the ministrations of a Catholic priest. Nikolai Lenin, as he lay on his deathbed, looked around him and frantically asked pardon of the tables and chairs in the room. For as hunger for food proclaims the existence of food, man's intuitive hunger for God proclaims the Reality, the Omnipotence and the Justice of God. Catholic belief in God, therefore, is purely and simply an expression of intellectual sanity.

Why do Catholics believe that God is three Persons, called the Holy Trinity? How can God be three Persons and still be one God?

Catholics believe there is one God consisting of three distinct and equal divine Persons—Father, Son and Holy Spirit—because on numerous occasions God has described Himself thus. The Old Testament gives intimations that there are more than one Person in God. In *Genesis* 1:26, God says, "Let us make man to our image and likeness." In *Isaias* 9:6-7, God the Father revealed the imminent coming into the world of God the Son. In *Psalms* 2:7, we read, "The Lord hath said to me: Thou art my son, this day have I begotten thee." And in the New Testament, God reveals this doctrine even more clearly. For example, at the baptism of Jesus Christ, the Holy Spirit appeared in the form of a dove, and the voice of God the Father was heard: "This is my beloved Son, in whom I am well pleased." (*Matt.* 3:16-17). In *Matthew* 28:19, God the Son commanded the Apostles to baptize "in the name of the Father, and of the Son, and of the Holy Ghost." And in *1 Cor.* 12:4-6, the Bible refers to God with three names: Spirit, Lord, and God—corresponding to the Father, the Son, and the Holy Spirit.

Three divine Persons in one Godhead may be incomprehensible to the human mind, but that is to be expected. How can man fully comprehend God's infinite make-up when he cannot fully comprehend his own finite make-up? We have to take God's word for it. Also, we can satisfy ourselves as to the feasibility of God's triune make-up by considering various other triune realities. The triangle, for example, is one distinct form with three distinct and equal sides. And the clover leaf is one leaf with three distinct and equal petals. There are many physical trinities on earth, therefore a Spiritual Trinity, who is God in Heaven, is not against human reason—it is simply *above* human reason.

Why do Catholics believe that Jesus Christ was God the Son—the Second Person of the Holy Trinity? Would it not be more reasonable to believe that He was a great and holy man ... a religious leader of exceptional talent and dedication ... a prophet?

Catholics believe that Jesus was God the Son, incarnate in human flesh, firstly because God's

6

physical manifestation on earth, plus all the circumstances of that manifestation, were prophesied time and again in Divine Revelation, and Jesus fulfilled that prophecy right to the letter; secondly, because He claimed that He was God (*John* 10:30, 14:9-10 *and numerous other passages*), and He never deceived anyone; thirdly, because He *proved* His divinity by His impeccable holiness and the flawless perfection of His doctrine; fourthly, because only God could have performed the miracles He performed—miracles such as walking on the sea, feeding five thousand people with five loaves of bread and two fish, and, after His death on the Cross, resurrecting Himself from His own tomb; fifthly, because only God could have, in the brief space of three years, without military conquest, without political power, without writing a single line or traveling more than a few score miles, so profoundly affected the course of human events; sixthly, because only God can instill in the soul of man the grace and the peace and the assurance of eternal salvation that Jesus instills.

Why do Catholics believe that their Church is the one true Church of Jesus Christ? Wouldn't it be more reasonable to believe that Christ's true Church is a spiritual union of all Christian denominations?

Catholics believe that theirs is the one true Church of Jesus Christ, firstly, because theirs is the only Christian Church that goes back in history to the time of Christ; secondly, because theirs is the only Christian Church which possesses the invincible unity, the intrinsic holiness, the continual universality and the indisputable apostolicity which Christ said would distinguish His true Church; and thirdly, because the Apostles and primitive Church Fathers, who certainly were members of Christ's true Church, all professed membership in this same Catholic Church *(See Apostles' Creed* and the *Primitive Christian letters)*. Wrote Ignatius of Antioch, illustrious Church Father of the first century: "Where the Bishop is, there let the multitude of believers be; even as where Jesus is, there is the Catholic Church." Our Lord said: "There shall be one fold and one shepherd, yet it is well known that the various Christian denominations cannot agree on what Christ actually taught. Since Christ roundly condemned interdenominationalism ("And if a house be divided against itself, that house cannot stand." *Mark* 3:25), Catholics cannot believe that He would ever sanction it in His Church.

Why do Catholics refuse to concede that their church became doctrinally corrupt in the Middle Ages, necessitating the Protestant Reformation?

Catholics refuse to concede such a thing out of faith in Jesus Christ. Christ solemnly pledged that the gates of Hell would never prevail against His Church (*Matt.* 16:18), and He solemnly promised that after His Ascension into Heaven He would send His Church "another Paraclete ... the spirit of truth," to dwell with it forever (*John* 14:16-17), and He inspired the Apostle Paul to describe His Church as "the pillar and ground of the truth." (*1 Tim.* 3:15). If the Catholic Church (which Protestants admit was the true Church of Jesus Christ before Luther's revolt) became doctrinally corrupt as alleged, it would mean that the gates of Hell had prevailed against it—it would mean that Christ had deceived His followers. Believing Christ to be the very essence of truth and integrity, Catholics cannot in conscience believe that He could be guilty of such deception. Another thing: Catholics cannot see how the division of Christianity into hundreds of rival camps and doctrinal variations can be called a "reformation" of the Christian Church. In the Catholic mind, hundreds of conflicting interpretations of Christ's teachings do not add up to a true interpretation of Christ's teachings.

If the Catholic Church never fell into error, how explain the worldly Popes, the bloody Inquisitions, the selling of indulgences and the invention of new doctrines?

A careful, objective investigation of Catholic history will disclose these facts: The so-called worldly popes of the Middle Ages—three in number—were certainly guilty of extravagant pomposity, nepotism and other indiscretions and sins which were not in keeping with the dignity of their high church office—but they certainly were not guilty of licentious conduct while in office, nor were they guilty of altering any part of the Church's Christ-given deposit of faith. The so-called bloody Inquisitions, which were initiated by the civil governments of France and Spain for the purpose of ferreting out Moslems and Jews who were causing social havoc by posing as faithful Catholic citizens—even as priests and bishops—were indeed approved by the Church. (Non-Catholics who admitted they were non-Catholics were left alone by the Inquisition.) And the vast majority of those questioned by the Inquisition (including St. Teresa of Avila) were completely cleared. Nevertheless, the popes roundly condemned the proceedings when they saw justice giving way to cruel abuses, and it was this insistent condemnation by the popes which finally put an end to the Inquisitions.

The so-called selling of indulgences positively did not involve any "selling"—it involved the *granting* of the spiritual favor of an indulgence (which is the remission of the debt of temporal punishment for already-forgiven sins) in return for the giving of alms to the Church for the building of Christendom's greatest house of prayer—St. Peter's Basilica in Rome. One must understand with regard to indulgences that there are always *two* acts to be fulfilled by the one gaining the indulgence: 1) doing the deed (e.g., alms-giving) and 2) saying of some prescribed prayers with proper spiritual dispositions. In the case in point, the first act for gaining the indulgence was "giving alms." If the almsgiver thereafter failed to say the requisite prayers, he would not receive the indulgence because he had failed to fulfill both required acts. The indulgences therefore were not "sold"; the very giving of money was itself the first of two requisite acts for gaining the indulgence in question.

The so-called invention of new doctrines, which refers to the Church's proclamation of new dogmas, is the most baseless and ridiculous charge of all—for those "new" dogmas of the Church were actually old doctrines dating back to the beginning of Christianity. In proclaiming them to be dogmas, the Church merely emphasized their importance to the Faith and affirmed that they are, in truth, part and parcel of divine revelation. The Catholic Church followed the same procedure when, in the fourth century, she proclaimed the New Testament to be divinely revealed. Hence it is obvious that the Catholic Church did NOT fall into error during the Middle Ages as some people allege, for if she had, she could not have produced those hundreds of medieval saints—saints the calibre of St. Francis, St. Bernard, St. Bonaventure, St. Clare, St. Anthony, St. John of the Cross, St. Thomas Aquinas, St. Elizabeth and St. Vincent Ferrer (who performed an estimated 40,000 miracles).

Why do Catholics believe that Peter the Apostle was the first Pope, when the word "Pope" doesn't even appear in Catholic Bibles? Just where does the Pope get his authority to rule over the Catholic Church?

True, the word "Pope" doesn't appear in the Bible—but then neither do the words "Trinity," "Incarnation," "Ascension" and "Bible" appear in the Bible. However, they are referred to by other names. The Bible, for example, is referred to as "Scripture." The Pope, which means *head bishop* of the Church, is referred to as the "rock" of the Church, or as the "shepherd" of the Church. Christ used that terminology when He appointed the Apostle Peter the first head bishop of His Church, saying: "Blessed art thou, Simon Bar-Jona . . . Thou art Peter, and upon this rock I will build my church." (*Matt.* 16:17-19). "There shall be one fold and one shepherd." (*John* 10:16). "Feed my lambs . . . feed my sheep." (*John* 21:15-17). The words "rock" and "shepherd" must apply to Peter, and they must distinguish him as the head Apostle, otherwise Christ's statements are so ambiguous as to be meaningless. Certainly the other Apostles understood that Peter had authority from Christ to lead the Church, for they gave him the presiding place every time they assembled in council (*Acts* 1:15, 5:1-10), and they placed his name first every time they listed the names of the Apostles. (*Matt.* 10:2, *Mark* 3:16, *Luke* 6:13-14, *Acts* 1:13).

In addition, there is the testimony of the Church Fathers. In the second century St. Hegessipus compiled a list of Popes to the time of Anicetus (eleventh Pope) which contained the name of St. Peter as first. Early in the third century the historian Caius wrote that Pope Victor was "the thirteenth Bishop of Rome from Peter." In the middle of the third century St. Cyprian related that Cornelius (twenty-first Pope) "mounted the lofty summit of the priesthood . . . the place of Peter." Even Protestant historians have attested to Peter's role as first Bishop of Rome, first Pope of the Catholic Church. Wrote the eminent Protestant historian Cave in his *Historia Literaria:* "That Peter was at Rome, and held the See there for some time, we fearlessly affirm with the whole multitude of the ancients." Hence the source of the Pope's authority to rule over the Catholic Church is quite obvious: It was given him by none other than Jesus Christ—by God Himself.

Why do Catholics believe the Pope is infallible in his teachings when he is a human being,

with a finite human intellect, like the rest of us? What is the scriptural basis for this belief?

The doctrine of Papal Infallibility does not mean the Pope is always right in all his *personal* teachings. Catholics are quite aware that, despite his great learning, the Pope is very much a human being and therefore liable to commit human error. On some subjects, like sports and manufacturing, his judgment is liable to be very faulty. The doctrine simply means that the Pope is divinely protected from error when, acting in his official capacity as chief shepherd of the Catholic fold, he promulgates a decision which is binding on the conscience of all Catholics throughout the world. In other words, his infallibility is limited to his specialty—the Faith of Jesus Christ.

In order for the Pope to be infallible on a particular statement, however, four conditions must apply: 1) he must be speaking *ex cathedra . . .* that is, "from the Chair" of Peter, or in other words, *officially,* as head of the entire Church; 2) the decision must be for the *whole* Church; 3) it must be on a matter of faith or morals; 4) the Pope must have the intention of making a final decision on a teaching of faith or morals, so that it is to be held by all the faithful. It must be interpretive, not originative; *the Pope has no authority to originate new doctrine.* He is not the author of revelation—only its guardian and expounder. He has no power to distort a single word of Scripture, or change one iota of divine tradition. His infallibility is limited strictly to the province of doctrinal interpretation, and it is used quite rarely. It is used in order to clarify, to "define," some point of the ancient Christian tradition. It is the infallibility of which Christ spoke when He said to Peter, the first Pope: "I will give to thee the keys of the kingdom of heaven. And whatsoever thou shalt bind upon earth, it shall be bound also in heaven." (*Matt.* 16:19). Certainly Christ would not have admonished His followers to "hear the church" (*Matt.* 18:17) without somehow making certain that what they heard was the truth—without somehow making the teaching magisterium of His Church infallible.

For a complete understanding of the Pope's infallibility, however, one more thing should be known: *His* ex cathedra *decisions are not the result of his own private deliberations.* They are the result of many years—sometimes hundreds of years—of consultation with the other bishops and theologians of the Church. He is, in effect, voicing the belief of the *whole* Church. His infallibility is not his own private endowment, but rather an endowment of the entire Mystical Body of Christ. Indeed, the Pope's hands are tied with regard to the changing of Christian doctrine. No Pope has ever used his infallibility to change, add, or subtract any Christian teaching; this is because Our Lord promised to be with His Church until the end of the world. (*Matt.* 28:20). Protestant denominations, on the other hand, feel free to change their doctrines. For example, all Protestant denominations once taught that contraception was gravely sinful; but since 1930, when the Church of England's Lambeth Conference decided contraception was no longer a sin, virtually all Protestant ministers in the world have accepted this human decision and changed their teaching.

Why do Catholics believe in seven sacraments, while Protestants believe in only two? Exactly what is a sacrament, and what does it do for a person?

Catholics believe in seven sacraments because Christ instituted seven; because the Apostles and Church Fathers believed in seven; because the second Ecumenical Council of Lyons (1274) defined seven; and because the Ecumenical Council of Trent (1545-1563) confirmed seven. In short, the enumeration, seven, arises from the perpetual tradition of Christian belief—which explains why that enumeration is accepted not only by Catholics, but by all of the other ancient and semi-ancient Christian communities—Egyptian Coptic, Ethiopian Monophysite, Syrian Jacobite, Greek Orthodox and Russian Orthodox.

To understand what a sacrament is, and what it does for a person, one must know the correct, the traditional Christian, definition of a sacrament.

Properly defined, a sacrament is "an outward sign instituted by Christ to give grace" (holiness) to the soul...that is to say, it is a divinely prescribed ceremony of the Church in which the words and action combine to form what is at the same time both a sign of divine grace and a fount of divine grace. When this special grace—distinct from ordinary, inspirational grace—is imparted to the soul, the Holy Spirit of God is imparted to the soul, imbuing the soul with divine life, uniting the soul to Christ.

As the Scriptures point out, this grace is the grace of salvation—without it man is, in a very real sense, isolated from Christ. And as the Scriptures point out, Christ gave His Church seven sacraments to serve as well-springs of this ineffable, soul-saving grace, the grace which flows from His sacrifice on Calvary:

BAPTISM—the sacrament of spiritual rebirth through which we are made children of God and heirs of Heaven: *"Amen, amen I say to thee, unless a man be born again of water and the Holy Ghost, he cannot enter into the kingdom of God."* (*John* 3:5. Also see *Acts* 2:38, *Rom.* 6:2-6).

CONFIRMATION—the sacrament which confers the Holy Spirit to make us strong and perfect Christians and soldiers of Jesus Christ: *"Now when the apostles, who were in Jerusalem, had heard that Samaria had received the word of God, they sent unto them Peter and John. Who, when they were come, prayed for them, that they might receive the Holy Ghost. . . . Then they laid their hands upon them, and they received the Holy Ghost."* (*Acts* 8:14-17. Also see *Acts* 19:6).

The EUCHARIST—the sacrament, also known as Holy Communion, which nourishes the soul with the true Flesh and Blood, Soul and Divinity of Jesus, under the appearance, or sacramental veil, of bread and wine: *"And whilst they were eating, Jesus took bread; and blessing, broke, and gave to them, and said: Take ye. This is my body. And having taken the chalice, giving thanks, he gave it to them. And they all drank of it. And he said to them: This is my blood of the new testament, which shall be shed for many."* (*Mark* 14:22-24. Also see *Matt.* 26:26-28, *Luke* 22:19-20, *John* 6:52-54, *1 Cor.* 10:16).

PENANCE—the sacrament, also known as Confession, through which Christ forgives sin and restores the soul to grace: *"Receive ye the Holy Ghost. Whose sins you shall forgive, they are forgiven them; and whose sins you shall retain, they are retained."* (*John* 20:22-23. Also see *Matt.* 18:18).

EXTREME UNCTION—the sacrament, sometimes called the Last Anointing, which strengthens the sick and sanctifies the dying: *"Is any man sick among you? Let him bring in the priests of the church, and let them pray over him, anointing him with oil in the name of the Lord . . . and if he be in sins, they shall be forgiven him."* (*James* 5:14-15. Also see *Mark* 6:12-13).

HOLY ORDERS—the sacrament of ordination which empowers priests to offer the Holy Sacrifice of the Mass, administer the sacraments, and officiate over all the other proper affairs of the Church: *"For every high priest taken from among men, is ordained for men in the things that appertain to God, that he may offer up gifts and sacrifices for sins. . . . Neither doth any man take the honor to himself, but he that is called by God, as Aaron was."* (*Heb.* 5:1-4. Also see *Acts* 20:28, *1 Tim.* 4:14). Also: *"And taking bread, he gave thanks, and broke; and gave to them, saying: This is my body, which is given for you. Do this for a commemoration of me."* (*Luke* 22:19).

MATRIMONY—the sacrament which unites a man and woman in a holy and indissoluble bond: *"For this cause shall a man leave father and mother, and shall cleave to his wife, and they two shall be in one flesh. Therefore now they are not two, but one flesh. What therefore God hath joined together, let no man put asunder."* (*Matt.* 19:5-6. Also see *Mark* 10:7-9, *Eph.* 5:22-32).

There you have it, the Word of Christ and the example of the Apostles attesting both to the validity and the efficacy of the seven Sacraments of the Catholic Church. In truth, every one of them is an integral part of Christ's plan for man's eternal salvation.

Why does the Catholic Church discourage

Bible reading when, according to the Apostle, "All scripture, inspired of God, is profitable to teach . . . [and] to instruct in justice"? (*2 Tim*. 3:16).

If the Catholic Church discourages Bible reading, the Pope, the thousands of Catholic Bishops, and the many millions of Catholic lay people, are not aware of it. For the Popes have issued pastoral letters to the whole Church, called encyclicals, on the edifying effects of Bible reading. The Catholic Bible far outsells all other Christian Bibles worldwide. In fact, it has always been thus. The very first Christian Bible was produced by the Catholic Church—compiled by Catholic scholars of the 2nd and 3rd century and approved for general Christian use by the Catholic Councils of Hippo (393) and Carthage (397). The very first printed Bible was produced under the auspices of the Catholic Church—printed by the Catholic inventor of the printing press, Johannes Gutenberg. And the very first Bible with chapters and numbered verses was produced by the Catholic Church—the work of Stephen Langton, Cardinal Archbishop of Canterbury. It was this perennial Catholic devotion to the Bible which prompted Martin Luther—who certainly cannot be accused of Catholic favoritism—to write in his *Commentary on St. John:* "We are compelled to concede to the Papists that they have the Word of God, that we received it from them, and that without them we should have no knowledge of it at all."

If the Catholic Church really honors the Bible as the holy Word of God—if she really wants her members to become familiar with its truth—why in times past did she confiscate and burn so many Bibles?

The Bibles which were collected and burned by the Catholic Church in times past—notably the Wycliff and Tyndale Bibles—were faulty translations, and therefore, were *not* the holy Word of God. In other words, the Catholic Church collected and burned those "Bibles" precisely because she does honor the Bible, the *true* Bible, as the holy Word of God and wants her members to become familiar with its truths. Proof of this is seen in the fact that after those Bibles were collected and burned, they were replaced by accurate editions. There can be no doubt that the Wycliff and Tyndale translations were corrupt and therefore deserving of extinction, for no church has ever attempted to resurrect them. Nor can there be any doubt that the Bibles which replaced them were correct translations, because they have long been honored by both Protestants and Catholics.

Why does the Catholic Church base some of

her doctrines on tradition instead of basing them all on the Bible? Did Christ not tell the Pharisees that in holding to tradition they were transgressing the commandment of God? (*Matt. 15:3, Mark 7:9*).

Observe that in the Bible there are two kinds of religious tradition—human and divine. Observe that when Christ accused the Pharisees He was referring to "precepts of men" (*Mark* 7:7), to their *human* traditions. Christ wanted *divine* tradition preserved and honored because He made it part and parcel of the Christian deposit of faith— as the Apostle Paul affirmed: "Stand fast; and hold the traditions which you have learned, whether by word, or by our epistle." (*2 Thess.* 2:14. Also see *2 Thess.* 3:6). This divine tradition to which Paul refers—this revealed truth which was handed down by word rather than by letter— is the tradition upon which, along with Sacred Scripture, the Catholic Church bases her tenets of faith—as the primitive Christian Fathers affirmed. Wrote St. Augustine: "These traditions of the Christian name, therefore, so numerous, so powerful, and most dear, justly keep a believing man in the Catholic Church." The New Testament itself is a product of Christian tradition. Nowhere in the New Testament is there any mention of a New Testament.

Why do Catholics try to earn their own salva-

tion, despite the fact that salvation can only come as a free gift from Jesus Christ?

Catholics fully recognize that Jesus Christ died on the Cross for their sins and thus "opened the gates of Heaven," and that salvation is a free gift which no amount of human good deeds could ever earn. Catholics receive Christ's saving and sanctifying grace, and Christ Himself, into their souls when they are baptized. Yet they also know that Christ has established certain conditions for entry into eternal happiness in Heaven—for example, receiving His true Flesh and Blood (*John* 6:54) and keeping the commandments (*Matt.* 19:17). If a Christian refuses or neglects to obey Our Lord's commands in a grave matter (that is, if he commits a mortal sin), Our Lord will not remain dwelling in his soul; and if a Christian dies in that state, having driven his Lord from his soul by serious sin, he will not be saved. As St. Paul warned the Galatians with regard to certain sins: "They who do such things shall not obtain the kingdom of God." (*Gal.* 5:21). It must be added that Christ will always forgive and return to a sinner who approaches Him with sincerity in the Sacrament of Penance.

Catholics follow St. Paul, who did not think that his salvation was guaranteed once and for all at the moment he first received Christ into his soul; for he wrote: "I chastise my body, and bring it into subjection: lest perhaps, when I have preached to others, I myself should become a castaway." (*1 Cor.* 9:27). Also: "With fear and trembling work out your salvation. For it is God who worketh in you . . ." (*Phil.* 2:12-13). "And unto whomsoever much is given, of him much shall be required." (*Luke* 12:48). "He that shall persevere unto the end, he shall be saved." (*Matt.* 10:22). Nevertheless, Catholics realize that even the fulfilling of Our Lord's requirements for salvation is impossible without the free gift of His grace.

Why do Catholics believe that good works are necessary for salvation? Does not Paul say in *Romans* 3:28 that faith alone justifies?

Catholics believe that faith and good works are both necessary for salvation, because such is the teaching of Jesus Christ. What Our Lord demands is "faith that worketh by charity." (*Gal.* 5:6). Read *Matthew* 25:31-46, which describes the Last Judgment as being based on works of charity. The first and greatest commandment, as given by Our Lord Himself, is to love the Lord God with all one's heart, mind, soul, and strength; and the second great commandment is to love one's neighbor as oneself. (*Mark* 12:30-31). When the rich young man asked Our Lord what he must do to gain eternal life, Our Lord answered: "Keep the commandments." (*Matt.* 19:17). Thus, although faith is the beginning, it is not the *complete* fulfillment of the will of God. Nowhere in the Bible is it written that faith alone justifies. When St. Paul wrote, "For we account a man to be justified by faith, without the works of the law," he was referring to works peculiar to the old Jewish Law, and he cited circumcision as an example.

The Catholic Church does NOT teach that purely human good works are meritorious for salvation; such works are NOT meritorious for salvation, according to her teaching. Only those good works performed when a person is in the state of grace—that is, as a branch drawing its spiritual life from the Vine which is Christ (*John* 15:4-6)—only *these* good deeds work toward our salvation, and they do so only by the grace of God and the merit of Jesus Christ. *These* good works, offered to God by a soul in the state of grace (i.e., free of mortal sin, with the Blessed Trinity dwelling in the soul), are thereby supernaturally meritorious *because they share in the work and in the merits of Christ.* Such supernatural good works will not only be rewarded by God, but are *necessary* for salvation.

St. Paul shows how the neglect of certain good works will send even a Christian believer to damnation: "But if any man have not care of his own, and especially of those of his house, he hath denied the faith, and is worse than an infidel." (*1 Tim.* 5:8). Our Lord tells us that if the Master (God) returns and finds His servant sinning, rather than performing works of obedience, He "shall separate him, and shall appoint him his

25

portion with unbelievers." (*Luke* 12:46).

Furthermore, Catholics know they will be rewarded in Heaven for their good works. Our Lord Himself said: "For the Son of man . . . will render to every man according to his works." (*Matt.* 16:27). "And whosoever shall give to drink to one of these little ones a cup of cold water only in the name of a disciple, amen I say to you, he shall not lose his reward." (*Matt.* 10:42). Catholics believe, following the Apostle Paul, that "every man shall receive his own reward, according to his own labor." (*1 Cor.* 3:8). "For God is not unjust, that he should forget your work, and the love which you have shown in his name, you who have ministered, and do minister to the saints." (*Heb.* 6:10). "I have fought a good fight, I have finished my course, I have kept the faith. As to the rest, there is laid up for me a crown of justice, which the Lord the just judge will render to me in that day: and not only to me, but to them also that love his coming." (*2 Tim.* 4:7-8).

Still, Catholics know that, strictly speaking, God never owes us anything. Even after obeying all God's commandments, we must still say: "We are unprofitable servants; we have done that which we ought to do." (*Luke* 17:10). As St. Augustine (5th century) stated: "All our good merits are wrought through grace, so that God, in crowning our merits, is crowning nothing but His gifts."

Had St. Paul meant that faith ruled out the necessity of good works for salvation, he would not have written: "... and if I should have all faith, so that I could remove mountains, and have not charity, I am nothing." (*1 Cor.* 13:2). If faith ruled out the necessity of good works for salvation, the Apostle James would not have written: "Do you see that by works a man is justified; and not by faith only? ... For even as the body without the spirit is dead; so also faith without works is dead." (*James* 2:24-26). Or: "What shall it profit, my brethren, if a man say he hath faith, but hath not works? Shall faith be able to save him?" (*James* 2:14). If faith ruled out the necessity of good works for salvation, the Apostle Peter would not have written: "Wherefore, brethren, labor the more, that by good works you may make sure your calling and election. For doing these things, you shall not sin at any time. For so an entrance shall be ministered to you abundantly into the everlasting kingdom of our Lord and Saviour Jesus Christ." (*2 Peter* 1:10-11). If faith ruled out the necessity of good works for salvation, the primitive Christian Fathers would not have advocated good works in such powerful words. Wrote St. Irenaeus, one of the most illustrious of the primitive Christian Fathers: "For what is the use of knowing the truth in word, while defiling the body and accomplishing the works of evil? Or what real good at all can bodily holiness do, if truth be not in the soul? For these two, faith and good works, rejoice in each other's

27

company, and agree together and fight side by side to set man in the Presence of God." *(Proof of the Apostolic Preaching).* Justification by faith alone is a new doctrine; it was unheard of in the Christian community before the sixteenth century.

Why do Catholics worship Mary as though she were a goddess, when it is clear in Scripture that she was not a supernatural being?

Catholics DO NOT worship Mary, the Mother of Christ—as though she were a deity. Of all the misconceptions about Catholic belief and practice, this one is the most absurd. Catholics are just as aware as Protestants that Mary was a human creature, and therefore not entitled to the honors which are reserved to God alone. What many non-Catholics mistake for adoration is a very profound love and veneration, nothing more. Mary is not adored, first because God forbids it, and secondly because the Canon Law of the Catholic Church, which is based on Divine Law, forbids it. Canon Law 1255 of the 1918 Codex strictly forbids adoration of anyone other than the Holy Trinity. However, Catholics do feel that Mary is entitled to a great measure of exaltation because, in choosing her as the Mother of Redemption, God Himself exalted her—exalted her more than any other human person before or since. Catholics heap tribute and honor on Mary because they earnestly desire to be "followers of God, as most dear children." (*Eph.* 5:1). Mary herself prophesied: "For behold from henceforth all generations shall call me blessed. Because he that is mighty, hath done great things to me; and holy is his name." (*Luke* 1:48-49). Catholics know that every bit of the glory they give to Mary redounds to the glory of her divine Son, just as Mary magnified God, not herself, when Elizabeth blessed her. (*Luke* 1:41-55). They know that the closer they draw to her, the closer they draw to Him who was born of her. In the year 434 St. Vincent of Lerins defended Christian devotion to Mary this way: "Therefore, may God forbid that anyone should attempt to defraud Holy Mary of her privilege of divine grace and her special glory. For by a unique favor of our Lord and God she is confessed to be the most true and most blessed Mother of God." Today 75% of all Christians still hold to this same view.

Why do Catholics pray to Mary and the saints when Sacred Scripture states that there is one Mediator between God and man—Christ Jesus? (*1 Tim.* 2:5).

When Catholics pray to Mary and the other saints in Heaven they are not bypassing Christ, whom they acknowledge as the sole Mediator between God and man. They are going to Christ *through* Mary and the other saints. They are asking Mary and other saints to *intercede* for them before the throne of Christ in Heaven. "For the continual prayer of a just man availeth much." (*James* 5:16). How much more availing is the unceasing prayer of the sinless Mother of Our Lord Jesus Christ! St. Paul asked his fellow Christians to intercede for him: "Brethren, pray for us." (*2 Thess.* 3:1). And again: "I beseech you therefore, brethren, through our Lord Jesus Christ, and by the charity of the Holy Ghost, that you help me in your prayers for me to God. . ." (*Rom.* 15:30). Christ must particularly approve of our going to Him through Mary, His Blessed Mother, because He chose to come to us through her. And at Cana, He performed His first miracle after a word from His Mother. (*John* 2:2-11).

It is clear in Sacred Scripture that the saints in Heaven will intercede for us before the throne of Christ if they are petitioned in prayer (*Apoc.* or *Rev.* 8:3-4), and it is clear in the records of primitive Christianity that the first Christians eagerly sought their intercession. Wrote St. John Chrysostom in the fourth century: "When thou perceivest that God is chastening thee, fly not to His enemies, but to His friends, the martyrs, the saints, and those who were pleasing to Him, and who have great power." If the saints have such power with God, how much more His own Mother.

Why do Catholics repeat the same prayer over and over again when they pray the Rosary? Is this not the vain repetition condemned by Christ in *Matthew* **6:7?**

Catholics DO NOT just repeat the same prayer over and over again when they pray the Rosary. The Rosary is a progression of many prayers—the Apostles' Creed, the Lord's Prayer, the Gloria, the Hail Mary and the Salve Regina—and these prayers are accompanied by many holy meditations. As the Rosary progresses, Catholics meditate on the joyful, the sorrowful, and the glorious mysteries of the life of Christ and His Mother. True, the Hail Mary is repeated many times during the course of the Rosary, and some of the other prayers are repeated several times, but this is not "vain" repetition, certainly not the vain repetition condemned by Our Lord. The vain repetition He condemned is that of people who pray standing "in the corners of the streets, that they may be seen by men."

No prayer is vain, no matter how often repeated, if it is sincere, for Christ Himself engaged in repetitious prayer in the Garden of Gethsemani (". . . he went again: and he prayed the third time, saying the selfsame word"—*Matt.* 26:39, 42, 44), and we are informed in the *Apocalypse* (*Revelations*) 4:8 that the angels in Heaven never cease repeating, night and day, the canticle: "Holy, Holy, Holy, Lord God Almighty, who was, and who is, and who is to come." The publican humbly repeated the prayer: "O God, be merciful to me, a sinner," and *he* went away justified; whereas the pharisee went home unjustified after his long-winded extemporaneous prayer. (*Lk.* 18:9-14). God was likewise pleased with the repetitious prayer of the three young men in the fiery furnace, whom He preserved miraculously untouched by the flames. (*Dan.* 3:52-90). Protestants also engage in repetitious prayer: the same prayers at mealtime grace, the same prayers at Benediction, etc. The time lapse is no factor; it is still repetitious.

Why do Catholics believe in a place between Heaven and Hell called Purgatory? Where is Purgatory mentioned in the Bible?

The main body of Christians have always believed in the existence of a place between Heaven and Hell where souls go to be punished for lesser sins and to repay the debt of temporal punishment for sins which have been forgiven. Even after Moses was forgiven by God, he was still punished for his sin. (*2 Kg.* or *2 Sam.* 12:13-14). The primitive Church Fathers regarded the doctrine of Purgatory as one of the basic tenets of the Christian faith. St. Augustine, one of the greatest doctors of the Church, said the doctrine of Purgatory "has been received from the

Fathers and it is observed by the Universal Church." True, the word "Purgatory" does not appear in the Bible, but a place where lesser sins are purged away and the soul is saved "yet so as by fire," is mentioned. (*1 Cor.* 3:15). Also, the Bible distinguishes between those who enter Heaven straightaway, calling them "the church of the firstborn" (*Heb.* 12:23), and those who enter after having undergone a purgation, calling them "the spirits of the just made perfect." (*Heb.* 12:23). Christ Himself stated: "Amen I say to thee, thou shalt not go out from thence till thou repay the last farthing." (*Matt.* 5:26). And: "Every idle word that men shall speak, they shall render an account for it in the day of judgment." (*Matt.* 12:36). These are obviously references to Purgatory. Further, the Second Book of Machabees (which was dropped from the Scriptures by the Protestant Reformers) says: "It is therefore a holy and wholesome thought to pray for the dead, that they may be loosed from sins." (*2 Mach.* 12:46). Ancient Christian tomb inscriptions from the second and third centuries frequently contain an appeal for prayers for the dead. In fact, the custom of praying for the dead—which is meaningless if there is no Purgatory—was universal among Christians for the fifteen centuries preceding the Protestant Reformation.

Furthermore, ordinary justice calls for a place of purgation between Heaven and Hell. Take our own courts of justice, for example. For major crimes a person is executed or sentenced to life imprisonment (Hell); for minor crimes a person is sentenced to temporary imprisonment for punishment and rehabilitation (Purgatory); for no crime at all a person is rewarded with the blessing of free citizenship (Heaven). If a thief steals some money, then regrets his deed and asks the victim for forgiveness, it is quite just for the victim to forgive him yet still insist on restitution. God, who is infinitely just, insists on holy restitution. This is made either in this life, by doing penance (*Matt.* 3:2; *Luke* 3:8, 13:3; *Apoc.* 3:2-3, 19), or in Purgatory.

Also, what Christian is there who, despite his faith in Christ and his sincere attempts to be Christlike, does not find sin and worldliness still in his heart? "For in many things we all offend." (*James* 3:2). Yet "there shall not enter into it [the new Jerusalem, Heaven] anything defiled." (*Apoc.* or *Rev.* 21:27). In Purgatory the soul is mercifully purified of all stain; there God carries out the work of spiritual purification which most Christians neglected and resisted on earth. It is important to remember that Catholics do not believe that Christ simply covers over their sinful souls, like covering a manure heap with a blanket of snow (Martin Luther's description of God's forgiveness). Rather, Christ insists that we *be* truly holy and sinless to the core of our souls. "Be you therefore perfect, as also your heavenly Father is perfect." (*Matt.* 5:48). This growth in sinlessness—in Christian virtue and holiness—is of course the work of an entire lifetime (and is possible *only* through the grace of God). With many this cleansing is completed only in Purgatory. If there is no Purgatory, but only Heaven for the perfect and Hell for the imperfect, then the vast majority of us are hoping in vain for life eternal in Heaven.

Why do Catholics confess their sins to priests? What makes them think that priests can absolve them of the guilt of their sins? Why don't they confess their sins directly to God as Protestants do?

Catholics confess their sins to priests because—as it is clearly stated in Sacred Scripture—God in the Person of Jesus Christ authorized the priests of His Church to hear confessions and empowered them to forgive sins in His Name. To the Apostles, the first priests of His Church, Christ said: "Peace be to you. As the Father hath sent me, I also send you. . . . Receive ye the Holy Ghost. Whose sins you shall forgive, they are forgiven them; and whose sins you shall retain, they are retained." (*John* 20:21-23). Then again: "Amen I say to you, whatsoever you shall bind upon earth, shall be bound also in heaven; and whatsoever you shall loose upon earth, shall be loosed also in heaven." (*Matt.* 18:18). In other

35

words, Catholics confess their sins to priests because priests are God's duly authorized *agents* in the world, representing Him in all matters pertaining to the ways and means of attaining eternal salvation. When Catholics confess their sins to a priest they ARE, in reality, confessing their sins to God, for God hears their confessions and it is He who, in the final analysis, does the forgiving. If their confessions are not sincere, their sins are not forgiven.

Furthermore, Catholics DO confess their sins directly to God as Protestants do: Catholics are taught to make an act of contrition at least every night before retiring, to ask God to forgive them their sins of that day. Catholics are also taught to say this same prayer of contrition if they should have the misfortune to commit a serious sin (called a "mortal sin" by Catholics).

Granting that priests do have the power to forgive sins in the name of God, what advantage does confessing one's sins to a priest have over confessing directly to God in private prayer?

Catholics see several advantages in confessing their sins to a priest in the Sacrament of Penance. First, there is the Church's *guarantee* of forgiveness, which private confessions do not provide; secondly, there is the sacramental grace which private confessions do not provide; and thirdly, there is the expert spiritual counseling which private confessions do not provide. With the Apostles, Catholics recognize that the Church is, in a mysterious way, the Body of Christ still living in the world (*Col.* 1:18); therefore they recognize that God will receive their pleas for mercy and forgiveness with far greater compassion if their pleas are voiced within the Church, in union with the Mystical Body of His Divine Son, than if they are voiced privately, independent of the Mystical Body of His Divine Son.

Do Catholics confess all the sordid details of their sins to the priest?

No, Catholics are instructed NOT to confess the sordid details of their sins, because it would serve no useful purpose. All that is required of the penitent is the number and classification of sins committed, as well as a sincere contrition for having sinned, a promise to make restitution if the sin has harmed others, a firm resolve to avoid future sins and the occasions of sin, and the carrying out of the penance assigned by the priest (usually the praying of a few prayers). Actually, there are fewer intimacies revealed to the priest in the confessional than are usually revealed to one's doctor, lawyer, or psychiatrist; hence the Sacrament of Penance is not the embarrassing experience many non-Catholics imagine it is. Rather, it is a wonderful *relieving* experience, for it is through this sacrament that sins committed after Baptism are washed away by the blood of Christ and the sinner becomes once again reconciled with God.

Why do Catholics believe that Christ is sacrificed in each and every Mass, when Scripture plainly states that He was sacrificed on Calvary once and for all?

Most non-Catholics do not realize it, but Christ Himself offered the first Mass at the Last Supper. At the Last Supper He offered (sacrificed) Himself to His Father in an unbloody manner, that is, under the form of bread and wine, in anticipation of His bloody sacrifice on the cross to be offered on the following day, Good Friday. In the Mass, not now by anticipation, but rather in retrospect, Christ continues to make that offering of Himself to His Father—by the hands of the priest. "And whilst they were at supper, Jesus took bread, and blessed, and broke: and gave to his disciples, and said: Take ye, and eat. This is my body. And taking the chalice, he gave thanks, and gave to them, saying: Drink ye all of this. For this is my blood of the new testament, which shall be shed for many unto remission of sins." (*Matt.* 26:26-28). Christ ordered His Church to perpetuate that sacrificial rite for the continued sanctification of His followers, saying, "Do this for a commemoration of me" (*Luke* 22:19)—so the Catholic Church complies with His order in the Mass. In other words, every Mass is a re-enactment of Our Lord's one sacrifice of Calvary. The Mass derives all its value from the Sacrifice of the Cross; the Mass is that same sacrifice, not another. It is not essentially a sacrifice offered by men (although men also join in), but rather it is the sacrifice of Jesus Christ.

Christ's bloody sacrifice on Calvary was accomplished "once" (*Heb.* 10:10), just as Scripture says. The Catholic Church likewise teaches that the sacrifice of the Cross was a complete and perfect sacrifice—offered "once." But the Apostle Paul—the same Apostle who wrote this text in the book of Hebrews—also bears witness that the sacrificial rite which Christ instituted at the Last Supper is to be *perpetuated*—and that it is not only important for man's sanctification, but is the principal factor in man's final redemption. In *1 Corinthians* 11:23-26, St. Paul tells how, at the Last Supper, Our Lord said: "This do ye, as often as you shall drink, for the commemoration of me. For as often as you shall eat this bread, and drink the chalice, you shall show the death of the Lord, until he come." Thus at every Mass the Christian has a new opportunity to worship God with this one perfect sacrifice and to "absorb" more of Christ's saving and sanctifying grace of Calvary. This grace is infinite, and the Christian should continuously grow in this grace until his death.

The reason the Mass is offered again and again is not from any imperfection in Christ, but from our imperfect capacity to receive.

Finally, the holy sacrifice of the Mass fulfills the Old Testament prophecy: "For from the rising of the sun even to the going down, my name is great among the Gentiles, and in every place there is sacrifice, and there is offered to my name a clean oblation: for my name is great among the Gentiles, saith the Lord of hosts." (*Mal.* 1:11). The Sacrifice of the Mass is offered every day throughout the world, and in every Mass the *only* truly "clean oblation" is offered, that is, Christ Himself; thus the Mass is the perfect fulfillment of this prophecy.

Why do Catholics believe their Holy Communion is the actual Flesh and Blood of Jesus Christ? Why don't they believe as Protestants do that Christ is only present symbolically, or spiritually, in the consecrated bread and wine?

Catholics believe that their Holy Communion, the Blessed Eucharist, is the actual Flesh and Blood of Jesus Christ, because that is what Christ said It was: "This is my body . . . This is my blood" (*Matt.* 26:26-28; see also *Luke* 22:19-20 and *Mark* 14:22-24); because that is what Christ said they must receive in order to have eternal life: ". . . Except you eat the flesh of the Son of man, and drink his blood, you shall not have life in you . . ." (*John* 6:48-52; 54-56); and because that is what the Apostles believed: "The chalice of benediction, which we bless, is it not the communion of the blood of Christ? And the bread, which we break, is it not the partaking of the body of the Lord?" (*1 Cor.* 10:16). "Therefore whosoever shall eat this bread, or drink the chalice of the Lord unworthily, shall be guilty of the body and of the blood of the Lord. But let a man prove himself: and so let him eat of that bread, and drink of the chalice. For he that eateth and drinketh unworthily, eateth and drinketh judgment to himself, not discerning the body of the Lord." (*1 Cor.* 11:27-29). Also, Catholics believe that Holy Communion is the actual Flesh and Blood of Jesus Christ because that is what ALL Christians believed until the advent of Protestantism in the 16th century.

Wrote Justin Martyr, illustrious Church Father of the second century: "This food is known among us as the Eucharist . . . We do not receive these things as common bread and common drink; but as Jesus Christ our Saviour, being made flesh by the Word of God." Wrote St. Cyril of Jerusalem, venerable Church Father of the fourth century: "Since then Christ has declared and said of the bread, 'This is my Body,' who after that will venture to doubt? And seeing that He has affirmed and said, 'This is my Blood,' who will raise a question and say it is not His Blood?" In

41

addition to the witness of Sacred Scripture and Christian tradition, Catholics have the witness of the Holy Eucharist itself: On numerous occasions great and awesome miracles have attended its display, and seldom has its reception by the Catholic faithful failed to produce in them a feeling of joyful union with their Lord and Saviour. In the face of all this evidence, Catholics could hardly be expected to adopt the Protestant position.

Why are Catholic lay people usually given Holy Communion only under the one form of bread? By not giving the consecrated bread AND wine, isn't the Catholic Church depriving its people of the full benefit of Holy Communion?

In the Catholic Church the congregation is usually given Holy Communion only under the one form of bread because, if the consecrated "bread" is accidently dropped on the floor in the serving, it can be wholly retrieved—particles of the Body of Christ would not be left on the floor to be desecrated. If Holy Communion were given under both forms, and if the consecrated "wine" were accidentally spilled on the floor in the serving, it would be a virtual impossibility to retrieve all of the precious Substance—some part of the Blood of Christ would, through smearing and absorption, inevitably be desecrated. By not giving the congregation Holy Communion under both forms, the Catholic Church is not cheating any-one, because in receiving EITHER the conse-crated "bread" OR the consecrated "wine," the communicant receives the complete Body of Christ, including His Flesh AND His Blood, His Soul and His Divinity. The consecrated "bread" by itself imparts a true Holy Communion with Christ, a full measure of sanctifying grace, even as Christ said: "The BREAD that I will give, is my flesh, for the life of the world. . . . He that eateth this BREAD, shall live for ever." (*John* 6:52,59). And the Apostle Paul: "Therefore whosoever shall eat this bread, OR drink the chalice of the Lord unworthily, shall be guilty of the body and of the blood of the Lord." (*1 Cor.* 11:27). After the Consecration the priest receives Holy Communion under both forms, and this suffices to complete the Holy Communion part of the Mass service.

Why is Latin the language of the Church? How can the congregation understand the Mass whenever it is said in Latin?

The Catholic Church began in the days of the Roman Empire, and the language spoken throughout that Empire was Latin. St. Peter moved the seat of Church government from Anti-och to Rome, and the Catholic Church govern-ment remains centered there to this very day. It was only natural that Latin became the language of the Church. As the centuries elapsed, for example, Latin still remained the language of the educated classes—even into the 18th and 19th centuries. Therefore, it is not at all surprising that Latin should still be the official language of the Catholic Church. It simply always has been. Furthermore, a universal language greatly facilitates the unity of the Church. Ecumenical Councils, for example, have always been held in Latin, enabling bishops from all over the world to communicate with each other easily.

Moreover, unlike English, French, German and the other languages of the Western world, Latin does not change over the centuries—it is not affected by national idioms, slang and the like— therefore, in Western countries Latin is the official language of the Mass because it helps to preserve the original purity of the Mass liturgy— although today, the Mass is usually said in the language of the people. Catholics have always had a complete translation of the Mass Latin in their missal, or Mass handbook, so they have always been able to understand and follow everything the priest says and does at the altar, even when the Mass is in Latin. It should also be borne in mind that the Mass is never exclusively in Latin. All sermons, Gospel and Epistle readings, parish announcements and closing prayers are in the language of the congregation.

Why do Catholics call their priests "Father" despite the fact that Christ said: "Call no man on earth your father; for one is your Father, who is in heaven"? (*Matt.* 23:9).

Catholics call their priests "Father" because in all matters pertaining to Christ's holy faith they perform the duties of a father, representing God. The priest is the agent of the Christian's *supernatural* birth and sustenance in the world. "Father" is a title which does not conflict in the slightest with Matthew 23:9. Christ forbids the Christian to acknowledge any fatherhood which conflicts with the Fatherhood of God—just as He commands the Christian to "hate" his father, mother, wife, and his own life, insofar as these conflict with the following of Christ. (*Luke* 14:26). But Christ does not forbid Christians to call His own representatives by the name of "Father." Catholic priests share in the priesthood of Jesus Christ (not a human priesthood), and their sacred ministry partakes of the Fatherhood of God. Like St. Paul (himself a Catholic priest), every Catholic priest can refer to the souls he has spiritually begotten as his *children in Christ.* (*1 Cor.* 4:14). St. Paul considered himself to be the spiritual father, *in Christ,* of the Corinthians: "For if you have ten thousand instructors in Christ, yet not many fathers. For in Christ Jesus, by the gospel, I have begotten you." (*1 Cor.* 4:15). The title of "Father" is entirely proper for an ordained priest of Jesus Christ.

Why do Catholics practice fasting and abstinence from meat on certain days? Does not St. Paul call abstaining from meats a "doctrine of devils"? (*1 Tim.* **4:1-3).**

Catholics give up eating meat—for example, on Good Friday—to commemorate and honor Christ's Sacrifice on that day, and to follow His instruction to deny ourselves, take up our cross, and follow Him. (*Matt.* 16:24; *Mk.* 8:34; *Lk.* 9:23). It is a practice that dates back to the earliest days of the Christian Church. Tertullian and Clement of Alexandria both mention it in their writings. It is a practice which is thoroughly Christian, for we note that Christ Himself recommended fasting, saying: "When thou fastest anoint thy head, and wash thy face . . . and thy Father, who seeth in secret, will repay thee." (*Matt.* 6:17-18). In the same vein the Apostle Paul described his own suffering for Christ: ". . . in hunger and thirst, in fastings often . . ." (*2 Cor.* 11:27). Fasting was practiced both by Christ's followers (*Acts* 14:22) and by Christ Himself. (*Matt.* 4:1-2). And Our Lord told His disciples that some devils cannot be cast out "but by prayer and fasting." (*Matt.* 17:20). Paul's denunciation of those who abstain from eating meat applies to those who reject the eating of meat entirely, as though it were evil in itself. His denunciation has nothing to do with the abstinence of Catholics, for on other days Catholics eat as much meat as do

46

other people. Moreover, the abstinence from meat is not binding on all Catholics. Young children, old people, sick people, and all Catholics in countries where meat is the principle diet, are excused.

Why don't Catholic priests marry? The Bible says that a bishop should be "blameless, the husband of one wife" (*1 Tim.* 3:2), which certainly indicates that Christ approves of marriage for the Christian clergy.

Catholic priests do not marry because, while Christ does indeed approve of marriage for the Christian clergy, He much prefers that they do not marry. He made this quite clear when He praised the Apostles for giving up "all" to follow Him, saying, "And every one that hath left house, or brethren, or sisters, or father, or mother, or wife, or children, or lands for my name's sake, shall receive an hundredfold, and shall possess life everlasting." (*Matt.* 19:27-29). The Apostle Paul explained why the unmarried state is preferable to the married state for the Christian clergy: "He that is without a wife, is solicitous for the things that belong to the Lord, how he may please God. But he that is with a wife, is solicitous for the things of the world, how he may please his wife: and he is divided." (*1 Cor.* 7:32-33). In other words, matrimony is good— Christ made it one of the holy sacraments of His

Church—but it is not conducive to that complete dedication which is incumbent upon those who submit themselves to another of Christ's holy sacraments—that of Holy Orders. Even so, the unmarried state of the Catholic priesthood is not an inflexible law—under certain conditions a priest may be dispensed from this law.

The Bible says that after Christ was baptized He "came out of the water" (*Matt.* 3:16), indicating that He was baptized by total immersion. Why doesn't the Catholic Church also baptize by total immersion instead of by pouring on the head?

The Catholic Church usually baptizes by pouring: 1) because water sufficient for total immersion is not readily obtainable in some localities, 2) because total immersion would be cruel for babies, fatal for some sick people and impossible for some prison inmates, and 3) because the Apostles baptized by pouring. In the *Didache,* composed by the Apostles, the following procedure for Baptism is prescribed: "Pour water three times on the head in the name of the Father, and of the Son, and of the Holy Spirit." The words "came out of the water" do not necessarily imply *total* immersion. They could just as well imply that Christ came up on the shore of the river Jordan after standing ankle deep in the water.

This is not to say that the Catholic Church considers Baptism by total immersion invalid—she simply does not consider it practical as a universal form.

Why does the Catholic Church baptize infants, who have no understanding of what is taking place?

The Catholic Church baptizes infants because Christ wills it. He must will it because He said, "Suffer the little children, and forbid them not to come to me." (*Matt.* 19:14). According to the Apostle Paul, one cannot truly come to Christ except through Baptism. (*Rom.* 6:3-4). Christ must will it because the Apostles baptized "all the people" (*Luke* 3:21) and whole households (*Acts* 16:15, *1 Cor.* 1:16). Certainly "all the people" and whole "households" included infants. Christ must will it because He stated categorically that Baptism is a necessary prerequisite for salvation (*John* 3:5), and He certainly desires the salvation of infants. He must will it because the primitive Christian Church, which had fresh firsthand knowledge of His Will, baptized infants. In the ancient catacombs of Rome the inscriptions on the tombs of infants make mention of their having been baptized. One such inscription reads: "Here rests Archillia, a newly-baptized; she was one year and five months old; died February 23rd."

An unbaptized infant is not simply in a "natural" state; it is in the state of reprobation, living under the reign of Satan, with the sin of Adam "staining" its soul. Therefore infants should be baptized as soon as is reasonably possible—usually within 2-3 weeks of birth. When children grow up with Our Lord dwelling in their souls, they have a powerful protection against sin. Moreover, Our Lord can thereby draw children to a deep love for Himself at a very early age—as He did with St. Therese, St. Maria Goretti, St. Dominic Savio, and Francisco and Jacinta Marto.

Why is the Catholic Church opposed to birth control? Where in the Bible is birth control condemned as being contrary to the Will of God?

The Catholic Church is not opposed to birth control when it is accomplished by natural means, by SELF control. She is opposed only to birth control by *artificial* means, by the employment of pills, condoms, IUD's, foams, jellies, sterilization, non-completion of the act of sexual union—or any other means used to prevent conception from resulting from this act—because such means profane the marital embrace and dishonor the marriage contract. God slew Onan for practicing contraception (*Gen.* 38:9-10); the word "onanism" derives from Onan's deed. In fact, up until the Church of England's Lambeth Conference of

50

1930, which accepted contraception and thus broke with the Christian tradition, contraception had been considered by ALL Christian churches, both Catholic and Protestant, to be gravely sinful. The Catholic Church does not feel free to change the law of God, as do Protestants.

In the New Testament, there is only one instance where sin is punished by God with immediate death; this was the fate of Ananias and Saphira, a husband and wife who went through the motions of giving a gift to God but fraudulently kept back part of it. The Bible says they lied to the Holy Spirit. (*Acts* 5:1-11). In contraception, two people go through the motions of an act of self-giving, but obstruct the natural fruition of their act, i.e., the conception of children, which is the ultimate purpose for which God created sexuality. Sexual union is a gift from God to the married, but by practicing contraception, married couples are accepting the pleasure God built into the act and yet denying Him its purpose, new people. They are in effect mocking God. But "Be not deceived, God is not mocked." (*Gal.* 6:7). Christ cursed the fig tree which, despite a fine external appearance, bore no fruit. (*Matt.* 21:19; *Mark* 11:14). Marriage is God's plan for populating Heaven, yet contracepting couples refuse Him the specific fruit of their marriage, which is children, when they engage in the act which should produce children yet frustrate the natural, God-intended result.

Further, the sin of "sorceries" or "witchcrafts"

("pharmakeia" in the Greek—*Gal.* 5:20; *Apoc.* 9:21; 21:8)—which the Bible condemns along with fornication, murder, idolatry, and other serious sins—very possibly includes secret potions mixed to prevent pregnancy or cause abortion. Such potions were known and used even in the first century.

Common sense and conscience both dictate that artificial birth control is not only a violation of the Natural Law but is a perfidious insult to the dignity of man himself. For it implies free reign to physical impulses; it implies total disregard for the fate of the human seed; it implies utter contempt for the honorable birth of fellow humans, those fellow humans who are born as the result of a contraceptive having failed and whose very existence is therefore considered to be an unfortunate "accident," rather than a gift of God; it implies the most extreme selfishness, for no advocate or practitioner of artificial birth control would have wanted it for his or her own parents. Further, contraception undermines the respect of husband and wife for each other and thereby loosens the marriage bond. Worst of all, many "contraceptives," such as the IUD and most if not all birth control pills, work by actually causing an abortion early in the pregnancy; thus, this so-called "contraception" is in reality abortion—the killing of a human being—rather than the preventing of conception.

In every age there is some favorite sin which is

accepted by "respectable" worldly Christians; in our times the "acceptable" sin is contraception—a sin which fits in perfectly with the view that the purpose of human life is to attain earthly happiness. The true Christian couple, on the other hand, will realize that God desires them to have children so that these children can come to know Him and love Him and be happy with Him eternally in Heaven. Marriage is God's plan for populating Heaven. How wise it is to let God plan one's family, since He loves children much more than do their earthly parents, and His plans for them go far beyond any plans of these parents. Innumerable stories are told of God's Providence to Christian parents who trusted in Him and obeyed His law. For those who have a true and serious need to space or limit the number of their children, the new methods of natural family planning based on periodic abstinence have proved to be extremely reliable (unlike the earlier "rhythm" methods).

Finally, the Christian will realize that the self-denial involved in bearing and raising Christian children is a school of Christlikeness. Our Lord said: "If any man will come after me, let him deny himself, and take up his cross, and follow me." (*Matt.* 16:24). But He also said: "My yoke is sweet and my burden light." (*Matt.* 11:30). God promises sufficient grace to those who seek to obey Him. And the resulting peace of soul which the obedient married couple enjoys is beyond all price.

Why does the Catholic Church make no exceptions when it comes to divorce? Does not the Bible say that Christ permitted divorce in case of fornication? (*Matthew* 19:9).

The Catholic Church makes no exceptions when it comes to divorce because Christ made no exceptions. When Christ was asked if it was lawful for a man to put away his wife "for every cause," He replied that a man "shall cleave to his wife, and they two shall be in one flesh . . . What therefore God hath joined together, let no man put asunder." (*Matt.* 19:3-6). And the Apostle Paul wrote: "But to them that are married, not I but the Lord commandeth, that the wife depart not from her husband. And if she depart, that she remain unmarried, or be reconciled to her husband. And let not the husband put away his wife." (*1 Cor.* 7:10-11). In *Matthew* 19:9 Christ does not permit divorce in cases of fornication. He permits SEPARATION. This is clear from the fact that those who separated were cautioned not to remarry. Read *Mark* 10:11-12 and *Luke* 16:18.

Also, we know that divorce is against Divine Law because it is plainly against right reason. Were it not for our man-made laws which "legalize," popularize, and even glamorize divorce, discontented married couples would make a more determined effort to reconcile their differences and live in peace; they would be obliged by necessity to swallow their false pride and accept the responsibilities they owe to their spouses, to their children, to society as a whole, and to God. Any sociologist will confirm that there is far less immorality, far less suicide, far fewer mental disorders and far less crime among peoples who reject divorce than among the so-called "progressives" who accept it.

Why have Catholic women traditionally worn hats in church? Are bareheaded women forbidden to enter Catholic churches?

The Apostle Paul explains that Catholic women should cover their heads while in church: "You yourselves judge: doth it become a woman, to pray unto God uncovered?" (*1 Cor.* 11:13). "Every man praying or prophesying with his head covered, disgraceth his head. But every woman praying or prophesying with her head not covered, disgraceth her head: for it is all one as if she were shaven...." (*1 Cor.* 11:4-5). Paul's words do not imply that the Church is closed to women who have no head covering immediately available, nor does the custom of the Catholic Church imply this.

Why must Catholics pay money for a Mass that is offered up for deceased relatives and friends when the Bible states that the gift of God

is not to be purchased with money? (*Acts* **8:20**).

Catholics are not compelled to pay for Masses offered up for someone's special intention. They are simply reminded that giving a "stipend" (usually $5) is the custom. Priests will oblige without a stipend being paid if the one making the request can ill afford it. Giving stipends for special intention Masses is the custom because it is only fitting and proper that there should be some token of appreciation for the special service rendered, especially in view of the fact that the average priest draws a very small salary. For many priests these stipends mean the difference between standard and sub-standard living conditions. And this custom definitely has scriptural approval. Wrote the Apostle Paul: "Who serveth as a soldier at any time, at his own charges? . . . Who feedeth the flock, and eateth not of the milk of the flock? . . . So also the Lord ordained that they who preach the gospel, should live by the gospel." (*1 Cor.* 9:7-14). Of course the gift of God is not to be purchased with money. But that does not imply that God's ministers are free-serving slaves. Protestants will generally agree to this because within Protestantism it is likewise customary to give the minister who performs baptisms, marriages, etc. a token of appreciation in the form of money. Protestants do not call their gift of money a stipend, but that is exactly what it is.

CONCLUSION

There it is—the truth about Catholic belief and practice. This is the truth which brought the author of this booklet into the Catholic Church . . . the truth which brings millions of people into the Catholic fold year after year . . . the truth which explains why Newman, Chesterton, Knox, Brownson, Maritain, Mann, Swinnerton, Muggeridge and a host of other world-famous intellectuals chose to embrace the Catholic Faith. This is the truth which inspired the following confession by the renowned scientist, John Deering—a confession which expresses in eloquent fashion the fundamental motivation of every Catholic convert, be he famous or unknown: "I was born and raised in an atmosphere of proud, agnostic intellectualism. My father, a medical doctor by profession, was a disciple of Schopenhauer and Freud, and my mother was an ardent disciple of my father. My own favorite dish as a youth was Voltaire. Thus by the time I reached manhood, I was quite thoroughly baptized in the pseudo-religious cult of humanism. I preferred to call it humanism because, unlike the blunt Voltaire, I never could profess publicly to being an out and out atheist, even though there really isn't much distinction between the two.

"Being of a curious, speculative turn of mind, with strong leanings toward the more challenging fields of dialectics, I eventually took up the study of metaphysics—the science of the fundamental causes and processes of things. This subject intrigued me, indeed obsessed me, as no other subject had before. Here, I told myself, was the *science of sciences.* Here was the supreme test of my personal philosophy. If God exists, I told myself, metaphysics would reveal Him. Either I would be justified in my quasi-atheism, or I would be compelled in conscience to abandon it completely.

"Then the inevitable happened. I came face to face with the proposition, proved by all the principles of logic, that God does indeed exist. The evidence was so abundant as to be incontrovertible. Just as sure as two and two make four, God not only exists, He IS existence. To argue the point would have been tantamount to arguing against all reality!

"Toppled at last from the vainglorious perch of agnosticism, I immediately set about making another intellectual ascent—this time up the great imposing structure of Christian theology. I procured a Bible and spent every free moment absorbed in its sacred content. I had established the existence of God in my mind; now I must know something of the nature, the *personality,* of God. The Bible, I figured, would give me a clue.

"Much of what I read in the Bible was vague—I was not, after all, familiar with the customs and language idioms of the ancient Jews who wrote the Bible—but I could grasp the central theme. Quite obviously, the central theme of the Bible portrayed

God not only as an Omnipotent, All-Intelligent Spiritual Being, but as the Essence of Love, Essence of Justice and Essence of Mercy. In other words, God is pre-eminently a *personal* Being. And Jesus Christ was God *personified,* come into the world not only to make atonement for the sin of Adam, but to reassert His Sovereignty, elaborate on His Laws and illuminate with brighter light the pathway to heavenly immortality. And the torchbearer of this light was His Church, founded on the Apostles. Endowed with the authority of God, and imbued with the Holy Spirit of God, His Church was given the holy task of perpetuating His ministry of salvation after His return to Heaven.

"There was the divine plan of redemption, life's real purpose, brought into clear and beautiful focus by the Author of the plan—God Himself. There, in brief, is man's only real hope for happiness and security.

"Only one thing remained to be solved. God's Church—Where amidst the vast galaxy of the world's churches was God's true Church to be found? Then I recalled something Christ said: 'Seek and ye shall find . . . knock and it will be opened unto you.' Inspired by these words of divine wisdom, I embarked on the search. I undertook an extensive study of comparative religion, concentrating on the Christian religions. Since the other religions rejected the divinity of Christ, they naturally were in default.

"With painstaking impartiality I held every

Christian church up to the light of Scripture, logic and history, checking and double-checking lest I overlook some small but significant piece of evidence. Three years of this meticulous checking, then I found the object of my search. I finished with one name superimposed in great bold letters on my conscience—*'Catholic!'*

"On every ground I found the claims of the Catholic religion valid and altogether irresistible. The Catholic Church is the oldest Christian church, I determined; therefore, she is the *original* Christian Church, the one Church founded, constituted and sanctioned by Jesus Christ Himself.

"I had no other recourse in conscience but to embrace the Catholic Faith. And now I must testify that it satisfies my mind, solaces my heart and gratifies my soul. My blessed Catholic Faith fills my soul with a peace and a sense of security I had never before thought possible.

"Now that I am in the Catholic Church I have a much clearer picture of its true image. I see in all her vitals the *Image of Christ.* In the reception of her sacraments I feel His comforting hand; in her pronouncements I hear His authoritative, cogent voice; in her manifold world-wide charities I see His love and compassion; in the way she is harassed and vilified I see His agony and humility on Calvary; in her worship I feel His Spirit girding my soul.

"This compels my obedience. All else is shifting sand."

Be sure to read . . .

CONFESSION OF A ROMAN CATHOLIC

by Paul Whitcomb

In this booklet, author Paul Whitcomb, a former Protestant minister, reveals how he was led to the Catholic Church by a thorough and studious reading and comparison of the Sacred Scriptures. Here he recounts the gripping, step-by-step process of spiritual puzzle-solving that finally culminated in his seeing that it is in fact the Roman Catholic Church which is the true Church of Jesus Christ—the Church which the Lord Himself founded upon Peter, the Prince of the Apostles, and which He promised to be with until the End of Time and against which "the gates of Hell" would not prevail; that it is that Church which continues to promulgate the selfsame Gospel of Jesus Christ since Our Divine Master ascended into Heaven. The author not only substantiates his arguments from the Bible, but shows in the process that it is *the Catholic Church and her teachings* which are based upon Scripture and not Protestant beliefs.

Quantity Discount

1	copy	1.50 each	
5	copies	1.00 each	5.00 total
10	copies	.90 each	9.00 total
25	copies	.80 each	20.00 total
50	copies	.70 each	35.00 total
100	copies	.60 each	60.00 total
500	copies	.50 each	250.00 total
1,000	copies	.40 each	400.00 total

Please see the inside front cover for Postage/Handling.

Order from—

TAN BOOKS AND PUBLISHERS, INC.
P.O. Box 424
Rockford, Illinois 61105